FISH LIGHT

Michael Waters

an Ithaca House book
Ithaca, N. Y.

Acknowledgment is made to the following magazines in which some of these poems first appeared: *The American Poetry Review, Four Quarters, Granite, The Iowa Review, La Huerta, New Letters, The Ohio Review, Rapport, Response: A Contemporary Jewish Review, Strivers' Row, Sumac* and *The Vanderbilt Poetry Review.*

"Politics" appeared on a postcard published by *The Stone Press.*

Some of these poems appeared in the pamphlet A RARE BREED OF ANTELOPE published by The Byron Press (England) in 1972.

Special thanks to John Skoyles for his help in the preparation of this manuscript, and to William Heyen and Al Poulin for their advice and encouragement.

ITHACA HOUSE, 108 North Plain Street, Ithaca, N.Y. 14850

Ithaca House books are distributed by Serendipity Books, 1790 Shattuck Ave., Berkeley, CA 94709.

for Robin

*'I am depressed and full of sad thoughts
tonight,' I say.
    And in her sympathy she makes no answer.
    'I love three things,' I say then. 'I
love a dream of love I once had, I love you,
and I love this patch of earth.'
    'And which do you love best?'
    'The dream.'*

—Knut Hamsun

A fish jumps, shaking out flakes of moonlight.

—Theodore Roethke

CONTENTS

I

____

THE DEAD   2
LEAVES & ASHES   4
FACING DEATH ON MAIN STREET   6
POEM TO AN INDIAN LAST SEEN
    FLOATING DOWN THE MISSISSIPPI   7
THE TIGHTROPE WALKER AT NIAGARA FALLS   8
GREYHOUND WOMAN   10
LATE ANGEL IN HAMMOND   12
INDEPENDENCE DAY   14
DISCOVERING AMERICA   16
LEAVING AMERICA   20

II

____

DACHAU MOON   24
NOTES FOR THE ATLANTIC BOTTLE   28
FISH LIGHT   30
THE FISH   31
THE ESKIMOS BUILD A TOTEM POLE   32
WORSHIPPING THE OAK   33
POLITICS   34
FOR THE COMING YEAR   35
OUR LADY OF THE VALKYRIES   36

III

NIGHT FISHING   40

HARVEST   41

WINTER STONE   44

INSIDE THE HOUSE   46

BEHIND THE HOUSE   47

SLEEPWALKER   48

THE RETURN   49

WEDDING POEM   50

LEARNING THE WAY   51

WINTER RETURN   52

POEM (FOR THE ROSES)   54

FISH LIGHT

THE DEAD

Maybe the dead are asleep,
it is certainly hard enough work.
I wake as if from winter,
a rosary of perspiration
staining my thin white lips.

On the farm nothing is easy.
All night I strain the tractor
to pull the stump into light.
So much is rotten here:
the sad green odor of mushrooms
like a stale air in the room.

Maybe this continues for life.

One morning the darkness
seems to root
somewhere in my legs,
and I leave the soul
in its warm bed of moss
and drive to the tree.

Nothing:
a few ducks taking water,
trailing their young,
like women who laugh at me.

So I imagine
the tree is not gone,
that young girls sunbathe
in its loving shade
on rising blankets of bread.

Who wouldn't give a picnic
to be enveloped in fog?

When the air
seems to press its skull
as a wafer on my face,
when the sky seems that close. . .

I think of it this way:

a tree is nothing
so much
as a belief in sleep,
in whatever rises from darkness.

LEAVES & ASHES
        for Michael Ryan

1
Sometimes,
when the bars close,
the streets seem to whisper in rain
like women mistaken for mother.

Her skin waves on a clothesline.
Her crotch bleeds over Chinatown.
The three graces of city life
moon in a doorway:

One is called *spare change.*
One is named *fire-in-the-trashcan.*
One resembles *death on a menu.*

Maybe the dark one
hauls you to her breast
like a blind lover on wedding night.

You would like to disappear.
You imagine dawn
opening your heart like a room.
Anyone could live there.

2
A thief can carry sorrow in his arms
like a daughter,
almost saved from drowning.
An uncle can be silent for years
You can wrestle your heart
at the nearest bar for a drink.

Suppose the memories hang on you
like a large coat,
an animal hugging your back.

How can you tell her to let go?
When you close your eyes
you imagine a winter sun
burning through mist,

or a young girl who wakes
to feel her breasts for the first time,
that look of surprise on her face,
like the magician
who discovers a strange bird in his coat.

FACING DEATH ON MAIN STREET

That winter, wearing a flannel shirt
so long the sleeves waved in the air
when any form of warmth drew near,
I often found myself reflected in the town
in windows that lined the street like ice.
Once, seeing a figure resembling a human
on the brink of some tremendous cry,
my arms waved like scythes under the lights
as if that lonely fellow would never die.

POEM TO AN INDIAN LAST SEEN
FLOATING DOWN THE MISSISSIPPI

Hearing about the boy who dove
into the Erie Canal, into even
a dead horse rotting the water,
I see you again and wonder
how you died, perhaps mangled
by a steamboat paddle or burned
at night by men who dropped you
with a splash into the muddy river.
Maybe you were drunk and felt nothing,
or else swallowed water until your lungs
burst with filth. Did you pass
a riverboat hauling negro jazz
from New Orleans as you drifted down
the Mississippi, huge catfish scavenging
your shadow for garbage? Or did you
turn, instead, into a dead horse
like so many water-logged objects
that boys throw rocks at or dive into?

THE TIGHTROPE WALKER AT NIAGARA FALLS
for J.B.

I could not eat for days.
Water flooded me like cold air,
the fear of an earthworm,
the easy flow of sainthood.

Something like a rope
ran through me
connecting me with the air.
I had nothing to fear:
death is an automobile,
a drive into the river,
a drive that freezes
each difficult breath in our throats.
Below me a body washed on stone,
pure and crystal,
clear enough to see through—
I did not look down.

There is a strange beauty here,
like a car
covered with a thin sheet of ice.
Once, inside a dark space,
I carefully rolled down each window
and stared through the ice.
Everything became so clear,
like my name arranged in a rock-garden.

I ascended,
wrapped like an angel in wings.
The air ran through my blood,
thickening the bones,
dark animals that cannot fly.
I began to walk for my life.

GREYHOUND WOMAN

Another night
spent along the poles,
shuttling between stops
like electricity,
the wind in the wires.
I feel unmoved
as the bus imagines speed
that tugs at the window
like a lost voice.
Tomorrow a repairman
falls to his death
from a call-box
suspended above the road.
I wear this bus
like a finger of silence
held to pressed lips.
All I have to tell
is the guilt of a woman,
her return to the flood
that carried Aunt Edna
down-river on a piano.
I held her close
as your next thought,
thinking with my hands
or not thinking at all.

Later, half-asleep in the depot
as the bus trailed into dark,
I imagined a row of line men
outside the window on payday,
and decided this next ride
wasn't worth it at all.

LATE ANGEL IN HAMMOND
      for Michael Sheridan

An angel lost here
might stir dust forever,
and a wing of ash settle
across the city like disease,
the death of romance.

Once this drive led to a woman
who burns like a sun above me,
blind in thick air.
She sings through my radio,
through my teeth.

Still the air is so dull
even the police are bored.
Huge semis jack-knife
while uniforms hunch over a radio,
listening for their deaths.
They know the last gifts of men
are worthless as their own sweet lives.

I pass them
and feel my own life wear short.

So as the heat shimmers like rain
I pull into a truck-stop
where a waitress resembling my angel
brings a glass
with a large screw drifting rust
across this dream-scape of water:
something I won't swallow
or ask her to return.
Her life is hard cash.

Honeymoon night,
spent counting the several tumbles,
my mind races ahead to a home
filled with the soft light of heaven,

only the stars resemble an accident
near the Indianapolis overpass
and a tired husband
not making it
for the last night in a row.

INDEPENDENCE DAY

In the hotel room,
the small-time businessman is sad.
He desires a new car more than sleep.
Something to do with women,
their legs the strong beams of light
thrown along the road. . .

Three accidents he tried to reach there,
driving fast, hoping to enter
into that hard relationship with the land.

He has lost track of the towns.
All night he imagines his daughter
who hasn't returned home in years—
she fish-tails for the boys in a runaway hearse,
the terror of the Long Island Expressway.

Maybe someone has placed a ring at last
on her stiff white finger.

* * *

Six in the morning,
the streetlamps are still lit.
One last drunk swims home in whiskey fog.
The businessman turns on the news. . .
more women who are sleek & sing
like seals stranded on a New York street.

His suitcase leans on the door.
Outside, the day is an alarm,
the smoke of romance
gone black, dead-set, against the sun.

DISCOVERING AMERICA

1
On the local radio station
one pure grace note
rings clean as violence
across the long hours,

an ambulance in the skull,

the skull grinning in the car
that shoots like a bullet
along the black ribbon of road,

the road like a scalpel
performing that impossible operation
on the diseased land:

sometimes it's hard to stop.

So to stay awake
this poet and I play games,
we guess the source:

Ella Fitzgerald breaking glass,
blues for a lost miner,
maybe a woman in the next town
dying in spite of our love.

Already I regret the breath
wasted on a woman in the last,
and although I've never been here—
this feels like a return.

Listening to the music,
I know the art of revival
spreads across the landscape
like a November frost:

for some reason it's easy
to imagine the heads of children
mistaken for oranges
in the silent groves of California.

2
So death surrounds us
like a civil defense warning,

the chorus of southern Ohio:

their throats the ripe fruit
ready to burst in your fingers.

We drive all night to Athens,
full of good news,

a long haul past the shanties
of abandoned school-buses,

where children rock their beds
to the slow tick of rain

3

I am with a poet who reads
the sequence of American women:

here they almost form a line,
it is that easy.

Later, in the motel,
making them scream all night,

a radio moans in darkness,
more children disappear in Texas,

orchards are lit by little faces
that burn like smudge-pots

for a reason

and the one pale woman
who holds my attention like the road

wears a thin black ribbon around her throat.

LEAVING AMERICA

Gulls wash a dune of stone,
weather-beaten & hollow,
the shape of an Indian's skull
seen clear across the water.

None of us has eaten for years.
The country drifts in the Pacific
and the landscape sways with dream.
Scavengers arrive like lice.

On the tracks an abandoned boxcar,
a few loose ties covered with weed,
something like a family.
So many forgotten lives to settle,

products of the California boom.
One railroad spike dangerous as gold
flashes violence on the horizon,
a razor tucked like money in a shoe.

There is still another country,
less romantic, where three men
who dragged a girl from her car
are killed on the tracks near Fresno.

Maybe a crazy brother, maybe a spike
in the brain, maybe, like Thoreau,
a railroad through the lungs
to carry a circus of loving geeks.

Feathers whirl in my ribcage too,
delicate birds leaving America.
I haven't the stomach for it.
A porcupine in love with himself

stands a better chance,
stumbling across this dark lawn.
Water breaks like history on the republic.
I am so full of good wishes and goodbyes.

ll

DACHAU MOON

1
There is a place like Germany in the body
that wants to remain a secret,
where all the tremendous weight of a life
is a kiss buried in the eyes,
pale moons that drift like heaven
across this bastard landscape

& I am flying to this place
on an overcast morning
when nothing is ready to rise,
so it's easy to imagine a moon
blue & romantic as a dead woman.

This country is full of surprises.
My parents have told me to keep an eye
for the family star,
the remains of dark bone charcoal
thumbed like a mole
on the left side of the forehead.

2
Three days in Munich
and my head begins to split,
the beer tastes like a railroad
& I have been too fucking polite
like a child come home from death.

I am astonished by the number of gold teeth
taken from the mouths of the dead
and placed in the heads of fine German women.
There is a beauty in gold
when found in a dark forgotten place

and a fear
when the moon resembles a gold tooth
lodged in the skull like a light.

The smile of the engineer is a killer,
precise as a military operation,
all the way to Dachau.

3

The stillness is so complete
not even the dead are here anymore.

All the fathers are gone,
having kissed their daughters like fever,
to a room where the moon is seen as a face
blue and almost romantic in mist.

So unlike the photograph in the museum:
someone, maybe an uncle,
strapped in a chair
with his forehead neatly sliced
& opened like a jewelry-box,
the brain and its still water
exposed to the hands. . .

His mouth shapes a small o
that could be a moon
disappearing for the last time.

4
The sad Jews
who may be our fathers
haul themselves across New York City
as if weighted with stones,

and in my pocket is a stone
selected that day in Dachau
that contains all the darkness of a family

and I remember the moon is a skullcap
not placed properly on the head
like this, Lord, like this.

NOTES FOR THE ATLANTIC BOTTLE

Too many days have passed
between shores,
dark shapes that drift
like moons
beneath the raft.
I am confused.

The water is calm,
an invitation to the deep
sleep of recognition.
I have returned
to a place of quiet disasters.
Small cuts in wood
have been made smooth.
There is no memory
of handling the knife.

The salt air presses
an invisible hand to my back,
the sign of a saint
more alone
than if he were by himself.

I look for something
that resembles me,
the secret of the past
resting just below the surface:
breath, movement,
the slow evolution of fish.
I have learned to walk on water.

Too many days have passed
and come to nothing.
I can no longer see myself,
the vision of great fish.
Somewhere beneath me
the dark dream of meaning
begins to rise.
I leave the raft
and walk away from this life.
Water forms a direction.

FISH LIGHT

            the pond's curve
past the petrified hearts of animals
that lay like love-stones on the pine floor

where I look for a face
in the marble light of a fish-scale.

*

I feel the old wound ache
and cast its shadow on the water

and hear the surge of one fish,
the snapper,
that swallowed my finger so long ago
and feels it nudging his heart in his warm ribs.

THE FISH
        for Lynne McMahon

It is something in the air
that doesn't belong,
like a fish, that makes us
hear ourselves from distances
as if we were under water.

We cast about for reasons:
the domed aquarium lights
the sky, a constellation
big as a city,
the hotbed of Atlantis.

Seeing it from below,
this huge fish or many
mouthing the same words,
the wind across the water,
we begin to speak
like the mysterious dolphins:
everyone understands us.

On clear night
we drift toward ourselves,
the sure movement of great fish.

THE ESKIMOS BUILD A TOTEM POLE

The head of a moose is wooden,
carved with teeth. Start here.
It will bring luck to hunters
and dogs. Next, frighten the enemy
with an evil spirit. Hollow a hole
through the mouth, let it whistle.
Make the eyes deep. Now an old face,
perhaps a toothless grandmother
left for bears on the tundra.
Eagle's wings and beak, the sour eye
of a fish, the breasts of a woman
shaped with bone. At the top,
your own image coated with the blood
of a seal. Grease the pole with fat.
Reindeer will lick it dry, the sun
make it flame. Praise it.

WORSHIPPING THE OAK

Tonight we will stop them.
Armed with pitchforks, ax-
handles and crosses, we cross
the tracks and enter the wood.

Now we can hear their chants,
and see them circling an oak,
a small flame at the root.
We know them all: the man

who won our votes last fall,
the woman who sells us grain,
those who work in the post office.
They have all been here before—

We will strike with the force
of lightning We will pile
the corpses under the tree
and build up the fire.

Then we will return home,
and sleep like gods,
and know we have done
the only thing men could do.

POLITICS

I tape coins on your nipples,
it helps me remember death.

When we make love,
the eyes of a president
rise along my chest.

FOR THE COMING YEAR

Kiss me like a daughter.
Soon I will be gone forever.
This train of winter snow

(wedding veil,
the pages of a diary,
soft petals of light)

disappears into your heart,
a coal black mountain.

In Pennsylvania,
where flowers bloom at night,
the face of my mother
races across the landscape,

in the shadow of crossed slats,
a swastika on her cheek.

OUR LADY OF THE VALKYRIES

I
St. Agnes, patron of the leech, vampire
Bat and expensive brothel,
Who would make a man go to hell
And back for a glimpse of fire

That would eat to his bone-marrow,
Have mercy. We are not giants.
Though we donate our blood to science,
Give it easily as a Pharaoh

Near death, we could not fill a hole
That has no bottom. Go ahead.
Unlike your giant who bled
Through stone for your love, stroll

To the edge of that rock and look
Down. Water crushes stone.
Take our bodies, leave our blood alone.
Be satisfied, Agnes, with all you once took.

II

St. Agnes with a rose: a thorn
Has broken from the stem.
It could not pierce your hand. Born
Feet first, you stand in Jerusalem

On snakeheads with a bare heel.
Is that what it takes to be a saint?
They finally broke you on the wheel.

Agnes, your picture dims my room
With its dark flower,
All I see at night. The power
Of the Load is in its last bloom.

III

NIGHT FISHING

There is a fish so large
the sky can't hold it,
these arms open wide
but the fish swims away. . .

and there is a land,
no bullshit,
where we can be happy
and hug our fathers, once,
before they die.

HARVEST

1
Leaving the bar,
maybe a mile of dark wood
or a century of snow,
these walks through the vague
gestures of windfall and willow,
my father places his face
like a leaf in my hair.

By moonflame, by foxfire,
by the sad green light of mushrooms,
by the nuzzle of bear
breathing its death in my face,

we make it, somehow, all the way home.

2
Strong as a farmer
drunk on the new hay,
he pulls off his leather boots,
brushes the leaves from my hair,

whispers *Last harvest is near*
and sleeps.

So I dream of my father,
fallen like a plow,

and discover a cave
deep in my own fresh soil,
releasing a cloud of bats,
enough to darken the sky
like some preacher's rain.

3
Next morning I tell my father.
He says
> *Once a farmer*
> *rigged a shotgun to the door,*
> *returned home, drunk,*
> *and blasted the bats*
> *clean out of his head,*
>
> *until he woke years later*
> *stunned in light,*
> *truckloads of wheat on the road,*
> *all the work done at last.*

We leave for the harvest.

WINTER STONE

I close my eyes.
Strange marriages
make the benches heave,
and something that rises
is always mistaken
for faith.

The cold authority
that lifts from stone
to shift the sad weight of trees
in high snow
is the voice of my father,
the only voice I know.

Only the statue is near—
why never someone who
loves me more than I do?

Today
I confess my feet are cold.
They are like deep roots
tangled in the web
of a great, sleeping spider.
I fear they are becoming stone.
Father, my life is like that.

This small package of flesh
begins to frost like a glass house.
How long has the owner been away?
I write my own fierce poetry
as if I could take his place.
Does it matter if I stay
or drive myself to return?
Lover, will I ever learn?

This winter
has the violence of a church.
Half my life has been spent
in this park,
as if I would see the statue fall.
I walk away from that life,
listening to the statue,
believing nothing at all.

INSIDE THE HOUSE

The table scares me,
it will soon go away.
I finger my knife,
pass the fear
down into my stomach.
So much like eating
I am no longer hungry.

The night air is deep
with currents,
a hanging man.
Soon the table will rise,
or a refrigerator
fall through the ceiling.

My lungs ache with the curtains.
This is what it means to be pure.
I try a poem,
something done often
like removing my clothes
when I'm home alone.

Only later,
thinking myself asleep,
do I begin to rise
along the thick rope
of my breath.

BEHIND THE HOUSE

I can hear the cattle of Asia.
In my backyard
they water in the mist.

Each odor reminds me:
bones rise and gather skin,
the white light of morning,
the rice of small farmers.
They stumble toward the city
like a solitary cow.

There are many ways to prepare
for death:
tattoo bones on the skin,
chant Indian mantras,
invoke every god we know.
I do not rise.

Small flowers bloom
on the sides of houses at night,
saints intent on confession,
and disappear by morning.
I sleep in the knowledge
we will return, less human,
the underbelly
of some white god, a cow.

SLEEPWALKER
        for Tony & Sandi Piccione

The thirst for that other life
somewhere behind me,
I descend into a cellar
with more bottles
when the darkness begins to move

off glass piled in one corner
of the brain, and I drop. . .
or wake to find my hands
speaking in a circular motion

as if cleaning glass. I
imagine rags, then water,
the tongue weaving its salt—
and I rise

to find myself in the cellar
where my hands have placed bottles
as if to show that sleep
doesn't touch them, where
night breaks through dark glass.

THE RETURN
    for John Logan

The one night I returned home, lost
for all good purposes and dry
as a bone to the woman who slept
without a single light burning,
I lay back-down on the lawn
and felt the grass rise beneath me.
This is a feeling I would die for:
being lifted like that to nowhere,
to a solitary hawk
that circled like one empty glove
in search of the hand that has disappeared
with familiarity. We could not land.
That bird would have come
if I whistled the right notes,
gathering its wings like children
to shoot me through the heart.
But I, spread-eagled below, nailed
to the lawn and still rising,
did not choose to move,
and passed out into that night
as into a waiting home.

WEDDING POEM

There have been days
when I felt my larger self
hovering around me,
an awkward angel.
We both enter you,
a spirit of flesh.

I don't mean to be
contradictory.
This is simpler:
one night, when I was drunk
and dirty from loving
another man's wife,
you took me, gently,
and washed my small bones with rice.

LEARNING THE WAY

The grasses have shed their color
like beautiful women in winter.
The landscape is sparse.
Missing you, I have walked out
thirty days in a row
to overturn the stones,
suggesting a calendar of grief.
These last days have been hardest.

Under the clay, red spiders
spin into their dizzy dance of solitude,
or a bare white circle stares back
like an eye suddenly opened.

Once, in the center of an eye,
a small blue stone
spoke to me of love,
having finally found the right word.

WINTER RETURN
      for David & Annie

Head bowed to darkness,
I recognize the tracks of animals
pressed in snow. Something recent,
a small bird touching on the field,
flying from my shadow
in the silence that occurs
between consciousness and not-knowing.

I keep Roethke's crow in mind,
so far back it hurts.
These prints are so full of emptiness.
I feel it surround me until I can't see
the lights of the house,
as if the house has suddenly disappeared.

Alone, full of something like ambition
to return some of this emptiness to my life,
I kneel in landscape
and press a circle around the last trace
of that delicate, scared-away bird,

touch the underbelly of the snow
until my fingers lift that emptiness
like my own life carefully into the air.
I carry that print toward the house,
my hands cupping a last egg of solitude
and bearing it like a gift to this world.

POEM (FOR THE ROSES)

The roses on the sill
are speaking to me of love:
their dark red petals
brush the panes with moisture,

bloom like dust in the mind's eye.
I am filling tall glasses
with clear fingers of water,
and arrange a fresh rose
by touch in each one.

This day, as the noon darkens
in partial eclipse,
I feel the half-light stir
the ghosts of dead roots,
as if I were on the verge. . . .

My sons drift in the yard
like trees planted last year,
and stare at the sun
through pinholes of cardboard.

I love those boys—
they are so stupid.
In raising their arms
they welcome this darkness
as they welcome age, or muscle.

Long shadows weaken the room
to a fine dusk; in the window
the roses flame the day to depth.
This half-world is already fading.
I try for us all to stare back the sun.